Francis Frith's
AROUND SHREWSBURY

◆

PHOTOGRAPHIC MEMORIES

Francis Frith's
AROUND SHREWSBURY

◆

Dorothy Nicolle

First published in the United Kingdom in 2000
by Frith Book Company Ltd

British Library Cataloguing in Publication Data

Around Shrewsbury
Dorothy Nicolle
ISBN 1-85937-110-8

Frith Book Company Ltd
Frith's Barn, Teffont,
Salisbury, Wiltshire SP3 5QP
Tel: +44 (0) 1722 716 376
Email: www.frithbook.co.uk or info@frithbook.co.uk

Printed and bound in Great Britain

CONTENTS

FRANCIS FRITH: *Victorian Pioneer*

FRANCIS FRITH, Victorian founder of the world-famous photographic archive, was a complex and multitudinous man. A devout Quaker and a highly successful Victorian businessman, he was both philosophic by nature and pioneering in outlook.

By 1855 Francis Frith had already established a wholesale grocery business in Liverpool, and sold it for the astonishing sum of £200,000, which is the equivalent today of over £15,000,000. Now a multi-millionaire, he was able to indulge his passion for travel. As a child he had pored over travel books written by early explorers, and his fancy and imagination had been stirred by family holidays to the sublime mountain regions of Wales and Scotland. 'What a land of spirit-stirring and enriching scenes and places!' he had written. He was to return to these scenes of grandeur in later years to 'recapture the thousands of vivid and tender memories', but with a different purpose. Now in his thirties, and captivated by the new science of photography, Frith set out on a series of pioneering journeys to the Nile regions that occupied him from 1856 until 1860.

INTRIGUE AND ADVENTURE

He took with him on his travels a specially-designed wicker carriage that acted as both dark-room and sleeping chamber. These far-flung journeys were packed with intrigue and adventure. In his life story, written when he was sixty-three, Frith tells of being held captive by bandits, and of fighting 'an awful midnight battle to the very point of surrender with a deadly pack of hungry, wild dogs'. Sporting flowing Arab costume, Frith arrived at Akaba by camel seventy years before Lawrence, where he encountered 'desert princes and rival sheikhs, blazing with jewel-hilted swords'.

During these extraordinary adventures he was assiduously exploring the desert regions bordering the Nile and patiently recording the antiquities and peoples with his camera. He was the first photographer to venture beyond the sixth cataract. Africa was still the mysterious 'Dark Continent', and Stanley and Livingstone's historic meeting was a decade into the future. The conditions for picture taking confound belief. He laboured for hours in his wicker dark-room in the sweltering heat of the desert, while the volatile chemicals fizzed dangerously in their trays. Often he was forced to work in remote tombs and caves where conditions were cooler. Back in London he exhibited his photographs and was 'rapturously cheered' by members of the Royal Society. His reputation as a photographer was made overnight. An eminent modern historian has likened their impact on the population of the time to that on our own generation of the first photographs taken on the surface of the moon.

VENTURE OF A LIFE-TIME

◆◆

Characteristically, Frith quickly spotted the opportunity to create a new business as a specialist publisher of photographs. He lived in an era of immense and sometimes violent change. For the poor in the early part of Victoria's reign work was a drudge and the hours long, and people had precious little free time to enjoy themselves.

Most had no transport other than a cart or gig at their disposal, and had not travelled far beyond the boundaries of their own town or village. However, by the 1870s, the railways had threaded their way across the country, and Bank Holidays and half-day Saturdays had been made obligatory by Act of Parliament. All of a sudden the ordinary working man and his family were able to enjoy days out and see a little more of the world.

With characteristic business acumen, Francis Frith foresaw that these new tourists would enjoy having souvenirs to commemorate their days out. In 1860 he married Mary Ann Rosling and set out with the intention of photographing every city, town and village in Britain. For the next thirty years he travelled the country by train and by pony and trap, producing fine photographs of seaside resorts and beauty spots that were keenly bought by millions of Victorians. These prints were painstakingly pasted into family albums and pored over during the dark nights of winter, rekindling precious memories of summer excursions.

THE RISE OF FRITH & CO

◆◆

Frith's studio was soon supplying retail shops all over the country. To meet the demand he gathered about him a small team of photographers, and published the work of independent artist-photographers of the calibre of Roger Fenton and Francis Bedford. In order to gain some understanding of the scale of Frith's business one only has to look at the catalogue issued by Frith & Co in 1886: it runs to some 670

pages, listing not only many thousands of views of the British Isles but also many photographs of most European countries, and China, Japan, the USA and Canada – note the sample page shown above from the hand-written *Frith & Co* ledgers detailing pictures taken. By 1890 Frith had created the greatest specialist photographic publishing company in the world, with over 2,000 outlets – more than the combined number that Boots and WH Smith have today! The picture on the right shows the *Frith & Co* display board at Ingleton in the Yorkshire Dales. Beautifully constructed with mahogany frame and gilt inserts, it could display up to a dozen local scenes.

POSTCARD BONANZA

The ever-popular holiday postcard we know today took many years to develop. In 1870 the Post Office issued the first plain cards, with a pre-printed stamp on one face. In 1894 they allowed other publishers' cards to be sent through the mail with an attached adhesive halfpenny stamp. Demand grew rapidly, and in 1895 a new size of postcard was permitted called the court card, but there was little room for illustration. In 1899, a year after Frith's death, a new card measuring 5.5 x 3.5 inches became the standard format, but it was not until 1902 that the divided back came into being, with address and message on one face and a full-size illustration on the other. *Frith & Co* were in the vanguard of postcard development, and Frith's sons Eustace and Cyril continued their father's monumental task, expanding the number of views offered to the public and recording more and more places in Britain, as the coasts and countryside were opened up to mass travel.

Francis Frith died in 1898 at his villa in Cannes, his great project still growing. The archive he created continued in business for another seventy years. By 1970 it contained over a third of a million pictures of 7,000 cities, towns and villages. The massive photographic record Frith has left to us stands as a living monument to a special and very remarkable man.

Frith's Archive: *A Unique Legacy*

FRANCIS FRITH'S legacy to us today is of immense significance and value, for the magnificent archive of evocative photographs he created provides a unique record of change in 7,000 cities, towns and villages throughout Britain over a century and more. Frith and his fellow studio photographers revisited locations many times down the years to update their views, compiling for us an enthralling and colourful pageant of British life and character.

We tend to think of Frith's sepia views of Britain as nostalgic, for most of us use them to conjure up memories of places in our own lives with which we have family associations. It often makes us forget that to Francis Frith they were records of daily life as it was actually being lived in the cities, towns and villages of his day. The Victorian age was one of great and often bewildering change for ordinary people, and though the pictures evoke an impression of slower times, life was as busy and hectic as it is today.

We are fortunate that Frith was a photographer of the people, dedicated to recording the minutiae of everyday life. For it is this sheer wealth of visual data, the painstaking chronicle of changes in dress, transport, street layouts, buildings, housing, engineering and landscape that captivates us so much today. His remarkable images offer us a powerful link with the past and with the lives of our ancestors.

TODAY'S TECHNOLOGY

Computers have now made it possible for Frith's many thousands of images to be accessed almost instantly. In the Frith archive today, each photograph is carefully 'digitised' then stored on a CD Rom. Frith archivists can locate a single photograph amongst thousands within seconds. Views can be catalogued and sorted under a variety of categories of place and content to the immediate benefit of researchers. Inexpensive reference prints can be created for them at the touch of a mouse button, and a wide range of books and other printed materials assembled and published for a wider, more general readership - in the next twelve months over a hundred Frith local history titles will be published! The

See Frith at www. frithbook.co.uk

day-to-day workings of the archive are very different from how they were in Francis Frith's time: imagine the herculean task of sorting through eleven tons of glass negatives as Frith had to do to locate a particular sequence of pictures! Yet the archive still prides itself on maintaining the same high standards of excellence laid down by Francis Frith, including the painstaking cataloguing and indexing of every view.

It is curious to reflect on how the internet now allows researchers in America and elsewhere greater instant access to the archive than Frith himself ever enjoyed. Many thousands of individual views can be called up on screen within seconds on one of the Frith internet sites, enabling people living continents away to revisit the streets of their ancestral home town, or view places in Britain where they have enjoyed holidays. Many overseas researchers welcome the chance to view special theme selections, such as transport, sports, costume and ancient monuments.

We are certain that Francis Frith would have heartily approved of these modern developments, for he himself was always working at the very limits of Victorian photographic technology.

THE VALUE OF THE ARCHIVE TODAY

Because of the benefits brought by the computer, Frith's images are increasingly studied by social historians, by researchers into genealogy and ancestory, by architects, town planners, and by teachers and schoolchildren involved in local history projects. In addition, the archive offers every one of us a unique opportunity to examine the places where we and our families have lived and worked down the years. Immensely successful in Frith's own era, the archive is now, a century and more on, entering a new phase of popularity.

THE PAST IN TUNE WITH THE FUTURE

Historians consider the Francis Frith Collection to be of prime national importance. It is the only archive of its kind remaining in private ownership and has been valued at a million pounds. However, this figure is now rapidly increasing as digital technology enables more and more people around the world to enjoy its benefits.

Francis Frith's archive is now housed in an historic timber barn in the beautiful village of Teffont in Wiltshire. Its founder would not recognize the archive office as it is today. In place of the many thousands of dusty boxes containing glass plate negatives and an all-pervading odour of photographic chemicals, there are now ranks of computer screens. He would be amazed to watch his images travelling round the world at unimaginable speeds through network and internet lines.

The archive's future is both bright and exciting. Francis Frith, with his unshakeable belief in making photographs available to the greatest number of people, would undoubtedly approve of what is being done today with his lifetime's work. His photographs, depicting our shared past, are now bringing pleasure and enlightenment to millions around the world a century and more after his death.

AROUND SHREWSBURY – *An Introduction*

NO-ONE KNOWS WHEN the town of Shrewsbury was first founded. Nor do we know when people first even settled in the area. It is unlikely that we will ever have the answers to these questions. However, there are some things that we do know; with a little bit of guesswork and lots of (fairly safe) assumptions we can imagine the town's early history.

In all likelihood the site was occupied from early times. Two thousand years ago there probably was a small community of Celts living and farming here.

Then the Romans arrived. Once they invaded Britain it was not long before their presence was felt everywhere. The Romans established a legionary fortress nearby from where they conquered the area that we now know as Wales. When the legionary army moved on to Chester, a civilian settlement took its place. Today we know this site as Wroxeter - the Romans knew it as Viroconium. Within two or three generations any Celts living in the area would have become quickly Romanised, and their small farmsteads would have had the advantage of a ready market nearby for any surplus produce. In fact, Viroconium was eventually to become the fourth largest town in Roman Britain. It had all the benefits that we associate with Roman civilisation - aqueducts, sewers, a hypocaust heating system serving a large bath-house and an excellent network of roads. This was most important of all, because this meant that there was a forum (or market place) bringing in traders from all over the Empire. Eventually in AD 410 the Romans had to abandon Britannia, but it is probable that the town of Viroconium served the local population for at least another 100 to 150 years before it, too, was abandoned.

The 6th and 7th centuries saw new settlers coming into the region from the east and south. These were Angles and Saxons coming, with their families and livestock, to settle and farm. Presumably some of these new people chose a relatively secure site where there was a hilltop almost completely surrounded by a river. It was an excellent site - safely above flood levels in winter and yet even in times of drought there would always have been water to drink and fish to eat. Also, and most important for the future growth of the settlement, the river served as a route for traders. Within a very short time this settlement grew. It has been suggested that an early church was established here possibly around AD 780 (St Chad's) to serve the growing population.

In fact, there may well have been two small communities living here - a religious one based on St Chad's church, and a more commercial, trading community living on the top of what is now Pride Hill. These settlements must have prospered, because in AD 901 (the first written reference to the town) a charter was signed here in which the settlement of 'Scrobbesbyrig' is described as a 'civitas'. The use of the word 'civitas' tells us that by 901 the settlement on the hill was already considered an urban centre of some importance. We also know that in the early 900s there was a mint in Shrewsbury producing coins - by law in those days mints could only be set up in well-defended sites such as towns.

The name Scrobbesbyrig tells us that in those days Shrewsbury must have been defended in some way, even if the defences only consisted of simple wooden palisades - the element 'bury' ('byrig') in a place name tells us this. But was does 'Scrobbes' mean? Many people have suggested that the town's name translates as 'the fortified place with the shrubs'. This explanation runs against most Saxon place names, where usually the first element is either a distinguishing feature about the place (what, after all, is different about a few shrubs?) or a person's name. I favour the explanation that there was a person by the name of Scrobb who settled here with his people and went about defending his homestead.

But how do you pronounce it? Today everyone argues about this, locals and visitors alike. Is it Shrowsbury or Shrewsbury? One has to

assume that early clerics tried to spell phonetically whatever they thought they heard: invariably in early documents the spelling included an 'o' or 'oe', so we can only assume that originally the town's name sounded more like Shrowsbury than Shrewsbury. So why did it ever change? We have no idea, but one local tradition has it that in around the 15th centu-

such castle was built at Shrewsbury and, in order to build it, over fifty properties in the town were demolished - a reminder, yet again, of how that little Saxon settlement would have spread over the hilltop. The castle we see today is probably much the same size as the original wooden castle on the site. Over the centuries it expanded: at one time its outer

ry a mapmaker simply made a spelling mistake, causing the argument which has persisted ever since. It is an argument that will continue, particularly as many local people nowadays often drop the 'r' and call their town Shewsbury instead.

Whatever it was called, by the time of the Norman invasion Shrewsbury was a thriving town, with several churches to serve its growing population. Soon after the conquest of 1066 the Norman overlords set about controlling their new territory with the building of castles to dominate their new subjects. One

bailey extended some distance up Castle Street, but by the time of the unification of England and Wales in the 16th century the need for a military stronghold here had ceased, and the castle had become much smaller.

Indeed, in earlier centuries the Welsh had often attacked the town. On several occasions they even managed to capture it and hold it for a few days at a time. This had been such a persistent problem that Henry III decreed that stone walls should be built all around the town. We must assume that there had always been defences of one sort or another before this time. Today the stone walls still survive, most notably along the street known as Town Walls. They also survive in the foundations of many buildings along Pride Hill. The walls were built in the 1240s, and by the 1260s merchants in the town felt so secure that along this street they began to build their town houses abutting the walls. Today evidence of these early medieval walls can still be seen in some of the shops here.

The merchants who built these houses were extremely wealthy and powerful. They were wool merchants, and it was their trade that made medieval Shrewsbury one of the wealthiest towns in England. As time went by the wool trade was replaced by the cloth trade, and to this day evidence of the wealth of these merchants can be seen in the many glorious timber buildings throughout the region.

But the good times could not last; on his visit to the town in 1642 Charles I 'borrowed' so much money from the townspeople in order to finance his army that he, and the army he stationed in the town, virtually bankrupted the local people. The town was later captured by the Roundhead army, but they were no better; so, when Charles II passed by in 1651, the gates were firmly closed to all sides, so that Charles and his Royalists moved on to Worcester - where they were totally defeated.

Later, the Industrial Revolution of the 18th century, kick-started just down the river in the area we now know as Ironbridge, brought many changes to the region, leading to rapid growth in the suburbs of Shrewsbury beyond the loop of the River Severn. Many factories were built: one of them, the flax mill in Ditherington, was the first iron-framed multi-storey building anywhere in the world - from it all the high-rise blocks around the world can be said to descend. It was not only in Ironbridge that innovations were being made.

The town also benefited from its site on the important stagecoach route linking London with northern Wales and the Holyhead route to Ireland. In the early 1800s this road was considered one of the most important in the country. But before long the railways began to appear. Shrewsbury was linked into the growing railway network in 1848; it became one of the major railway stations in the country, with some 180 trains passing through the station each day in the early 1900s - and that was just the passenger trains.

Rail travel brought increased movement of people all around the country; with it came the first 'tourists' in the modern sense, and, of course, the market for Francis Frith postcards. Today Shrewsbury is promoted throughout the world as a medieval or Tudor town, and tourists visiting the town are an important part of the local economy. But for those who live here, it still serves as our local market town with its centres for rural and light industry - albeit with a growing number of additional tourist 'industries' such as English language teaching.

Today as we approach the year 2001 and the 1100th anniversary (at least!) of that little Saxon town on a hilltop site surrounded by a river, we should not, however, just look back on our history. Shrewsbury is a beautiful town with much to offer both to visitors and people living locally; Shrewsbury people can look forward to the future with a great deal of optimism.

THE MARKET SQUARE 1891 28912

The Square is dominated by the statue of Robert Clive, Clive of India. Born in 1725, he joined the East India Company's army fighting the French for control of India. His greatest victory was at the Battle of Plassey in 1757. Clive's statue stands here because he was Mayor and also MP for Shrewsbury.

THE SQUARE 1901 47192A

Compare the timber building on the right with the photograph above - a third floor has just been added and the windows are more decorative. It has been so cleverly done that today this Victorian/Tudor mix tricks everyone. Notice also that the trees have gone - fortunately they are back again nowadays.

THE OLD MARKET HALL 1891 28913
This hall was built in 1596, and its upper floor served as a cloth market. Around 750,000 yards of woollen cloth would have been sold here each year. There is a superb crest on the building depicting the English lion and Welsh dragon, symbols of Elizabeth I during whose reign the hall was built.

THE OLD MARKET HALL AND PRINCESS STREET 1911 63226
Until recently the upper floor of the market hall was used as a magistrate's court. Today it stands empty as local people argue about what to do with the building.

LLOYD'S MANSION, PRINCESS STREET 1904 51360

Standing just beside the old Market Hall, Lloyd's Mansion was demolished in the 1930s - it would never be allowed today. Notice the superb carving detail all over the building and particularly along the gable end.

PEACOCK PASSAGE 1891 28922

PEACOCK PASSAGE 1891
This is one of the 'shuts' for which Shrewsbury is famous. A 'shut' is the local name for a narrow little passage linking two larger streets; there used to be around 200 of them in the town, but today only about 20 exist. Peacock Passage gets its name from an old inn.

◆

IRELAND'S MANSION 1891
This enormous townhouse was nicknamed 'Ireland's Folly' by local people when it was first built in the 1500s. It is an early example of speculative building: the one building was divided into three so that Ireland, the merchant who built it, could rent out the two end sections in order to help him with financing them all. Very astute.

IRELAND'S MANSION 1891 28915

IRELAND'S MANSION 1903

Nikolaus Pevsner describes this house as 'the only timber-framed house in Shrewsbury to which one might grant grandeur'. A bit unfair - although he has a point. Many people find it hard to believe it is genuine Tudor rather than a more recent fake, if only because of its size and position in the town centre.

HIGH STREET 1911

The timber houses here were built by wealthy cloth merchants in the late 1500s. R Maddox & Co is therefore continuing a tradition by selling cloth and clothing. The company also seems to offer a delivery service - it is just possible to make out their name on the cart in the foreground.

IRELAND'S MANSION 1903 49487

HIGH STREET 1911 63228

HIGH STREET 1923 73810

It is fun to see how transport changes in these photographs. Also a signpost has now appeared at the end of the street with, below it, a policeman directing traffic. There is another policeman at the same spot in the next photograph - perhaps it is the same man, for after all there is only eight years between the two pictures.

HIGH STREET 1931 83877

FISH STREET 1891 2892

HIGH STREET 1931
It is only eight years later, and yet the cars are so different. Today all the buildings are much the same, except for Lloyds Bank at the end of the street; it was replaced in the 1960s - it was, after all, only Victorian (!) whereas the other timber buildings here all date from the 16th century.

◆

FISH STREET 1891
Following recent restoration of the buildings on the left, Fish Street is now one of the quaintest and most photographed streets in Shrewsbury. Here, in medieval times, fish was sold, hence the street's name.

FISH STREET 1924 76181
It is no wonder that this street (without the telegraph pole!) was used as a set in the recent film of Charles Dickens' 'A Christmas Carol'. The house just beyond the steps was used as Bob Cratchett and Tiny Tim's house in the film.

THE OLD MINT 1891 28924
Today this doorway can still be seen - it is now an attractive interior wall in a dress shop! The building is locally known as the Old Mint because, in medieval times, a moneyer lived here for a time and stamped his coins here.

BUTCHER ROW 1891 28917

Recent research on this building, now known as the Abbot's House, has revealed that its timbers were cut down in 1457 and used immediately, and the building was completed in 1459 when a 'topping out ceremony' was held. Records of the party are still held in the town's archives.

BUTCHER ROW 1924 76179

Originally each of the windows on the ground floor would have been rented as individual butcher's booths. Imagine the noise as they tried to out-shout each other. Imagine the filth and stench. It was only in the 1820s that this area began to be cleaned up when Street Improvement Acts were introduced.

PRIDE HILL 1923 73812

There are some fascinating shop signs in this photo. On the left (behind the lady with the stick) is 'W Whittal. Family Butcher. English Meat Only'. Most appropriate these days. Others include [Si]nger Sewing Machines', 'Abdulla Cigarettes', 'All Kodak Supplies'.

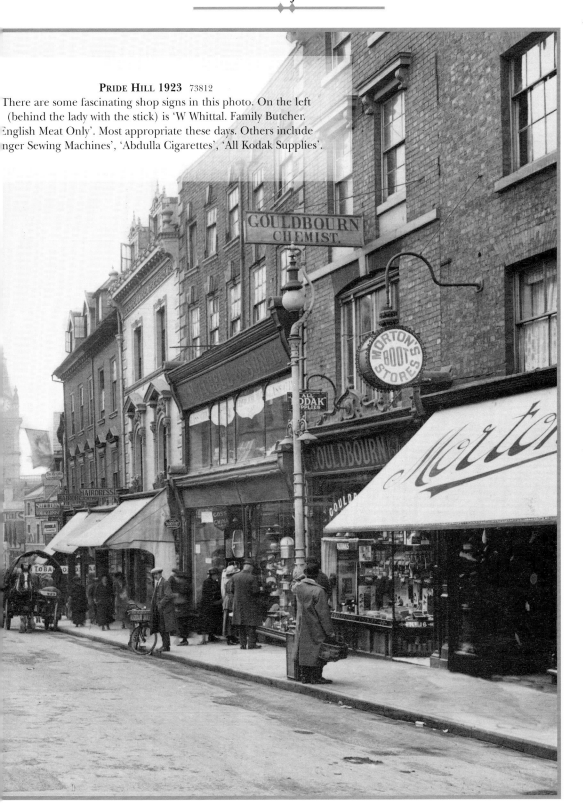

PRIDE HILL AND THE POST OFFICE 1891 28909

This photograph was taken further up the same street. It must have been a Sunday - all the shops are well shuttered up. The name Pride Hill came from a family of that name who lived here in the early 13th century. However, the name for the street does not appear in town records until two centuries later.

PRIDE HILL 1911 63225

In these photographs of Pride Hill, notice how the buildings on the right keep changing. There is only one car parked in the street. By the 1950s Pride Hill was totally clogged up with traffic; today it is the main pedestrianised shopping street in the town.

PRIDE HILL 1931 83881

PRIDE HILL 1931
FW Woolworth and Co Ltd has now replaced two former buildings. It proudly announces that it is a '3d and 6d store' - in other words everything in the shop cost either just over 1 or 2 pence in today's money! Since then Woolworth's has moved, and here we now have the entrance to the Darwin Shopping Centre.

◆

ST MARY'S CHURCH 1891
St Mary's is the oldest church building surviving within the heart of Shrewsbury. Its patchwork exterior with its mixture of red and white stone surprises visitors. Today we find stone churches attractive, and forget that when first built they would invariably have been plastered or whitewashed over.

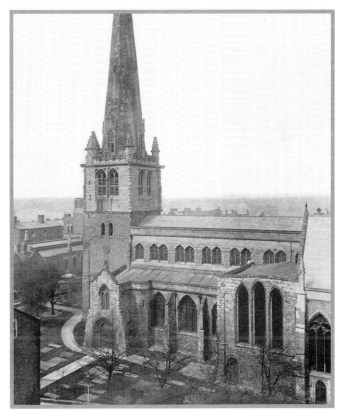

ST MARY'S CHURCH 1891 28931

ST MARY'S CHURCH PORCH 1891 28933

ST MARY'S CHURCH PORCH 1891

St Mary's was founded in Anglo-Saxon times, and the foundations of that church still exist under the present nave. Rebuilt in the 12th century, the church has been continuously enlarged and adorned, so that now we have architecture from nearly all periods represented here, as in so many of our historic churches.

ST MARY'S CHURCH
Jesse Window 1911

Although still a consecrated church, St Mary's is now redundant. However, it houses a fine collection of medieval stained glass from both England and Europe. The magnificent Jesse Window at the east end dates from around 1350, and has just been restored.

ST MARY'S CHURCH, JESSE WINDOW 1911 63247

THE FREE LIBRARY 1896 38098

Originally this was Shrewsbury School, founded in 1552. The section on the right was built in the 1590s, when the school was the largest in the country. The additional classrooms on the left were added in the 1620s. Notice the statues of two schoolboys over the entrance - they are wearing the costume of the time.

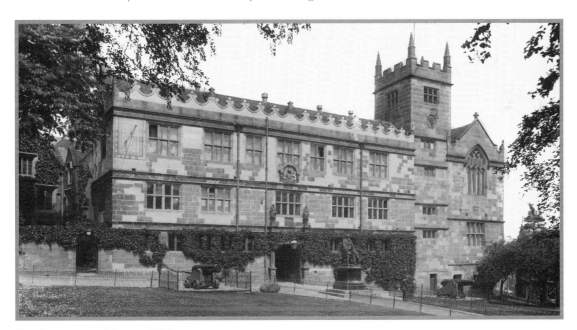

THE LIBRARY AND MUSEUM 1911 63253

Many famous people attended Shrewsbury School, including Sir Philip Sidney and Bloody Judge Jeffreys. The most famous, however, was Charles Darwin, whose statue sits outside the building. He attended from 1818; the other schoolboys nicknamed him 'Gas' when hearing of the chemistry experiments he carried out in his lab in a garden shed at home.

THE RAVEN HOTEL AND CASTLE STREET 1911 63223
Once one of the main hotels in the town, the Raven
was demolished in the 1960s to be replaced by the
bland architecture of Woolworth's In 1943 the hotel
became the American Red Cross Club, which was
opened on 4 July with 'a tea party very different from
the unhappy affair at Boston in 1773'.

THE CASTLE GATEWAY 1911
The first castle on this site was a wooden motte and bailey castle built soon after the Norman conquest. It was quickly replaced by a stone castle; it is thought that the only part of that first castle still to survive may be the Norman stonework of the entrance, seen here.

◆

THE CASTLE 1931
The castle was one of a series of castles in the area controlling the English/Welsh border. Originally owned by Roger de Montgomery, created 1st Earl of Shrewsbury by William I, it passed to his son Robert. Robert later rebelled against Henry I and so lost his English estates. The castle then became a royal castle.

THE CASTLE GATEWAY 1911 63254

THE CASTLE 1931 83861

THE CASTLE 1931 83862

Once England and Wales became (officially at least) one nation under the Tudors, many of the castles in the area ceased to be militarily important. This one, by then in a very derelict state, became a private house leased by Richard Onslow, who did much to restore the building at great personal expense.

THE CASTLE GROUNDS AND POSTERN GATE 1931 83864

Although now a very peaceful area with lovely gardens, the castle did see action once again during the Civil War. The postern gate pictured here was built during this period, when vain attempts were made to refortify the castle; it was captured soon afterwards by the Parliamentarian army.

THE CASTLE, LAURA'S TOWER FROM THE DOORWAY 1931 83868

By the late 1700s Shrewsbury Castle was owned by Sir William Pulteney, 'the richest commoner in England' at the time. He invited Thomas Telford to restore and modernise the castle as a private house. Telford even installed cisterns to provide running water for taps and toilets - very unusual in those days.

THE CASTLE
Laura's Tower 1931

Telford also built this summer house for Pulteney's daughter, Laura, on top of the old motte. Standing up here one can see in all directions and understand why Leland, the 16th-century antiquary, said 'the Towne of Shrewsbury standeth on a Rocky Hill of Stone'.

THE CASTLE
The Council Chamber 1931

Some years ago the castle was used for council offices, but in 1981 the council moved out; the building now houses the Shropshire Military Museum. One regiment commemorated here, the 85th Regiment of Light Infantry, was the one that burnt down the original White House in Washington in 1814.

THE CASTLE, LAURA'S TOWER 1931 83867

THE CASTLE, THE COUNCIL CHAMBER 1931 83865

THE RAILWAY STATION 1904 51362
This beautiful railway station was opened in 1848. Some fifty years later it was enlarged with the addition of a new floor inserted below the entire building - the original ground level entry was through what is now a window in this picture, just below the oriel window in the clock tower.

THE CASTLE 1891 28905

Below the castle, by the entrance to the railway station, it is the advertisements that attract attention once more. You are certainly encouraged to keep clean - 'Wright's coal tar soap', 'Sunlight soap', 'Matchless cleanser soap' and even the 'Droitwich Royal Brine Baths'!

THE CASTLE 1901 47193

Compare this photograph carefully with those opposite. A site office (the timber building on the left) has appeared, but the horses and carriages are still parked on the old ground level.

THE CASTLE 1903 49486

When the station was enlarged all the ground in front was dug away to allow access. This picture shows the old ground level (the road in front of T Wardley) and the new level where the horses and carriages now wait. Also, the workmen are still on site building the retaining wall on the left.

THE CASTLE c1960 S125088

Morris's cafe on the right was part of a large company still based in Shrewsbury. The first grocery store was founded in 1869 by John Kent Morris. By the early 1900s they had expanded, with interests in oil as well as groceries, bakeries and confectionery. Notice how often their buildings or advertisements appear in this book!

THE THEATRE ROYAL AND THE MARKET HALL 1931 83883
The market hall on the left was described by Pevsner as 'the chief Victorian contribution to public architecture in the town, and not one to be proud of'. Pevsner did like the clock tower, however. I wonder what he would think of the present market that sits here.

MARDOL 1891 28925

Mardol is thought to mean 'the devil's boundary'. Certainly it is a street leading out of the town (or towards the town's boundary), but we can only guess as to why the devil should be connected in any way. Notice Boylin's Umbrella Hospital on the right of the photograph.

ST CHAD'S CHURCH 1911 63233

Completed in 1792, St Chad's sits on the edge of the old town. It was described in 1897 as being in 'execrable taste', but I like it. The interior is wonderfully light and airy, with a gallery sitting on cast iron columns - a reminder of the industrial changes taking place locally when it was built.

THE WAR MEMORIAL 1911

A war memorial is a familiar sight in towns and villages all over the country. But notice the date - 1911. This is in fact a memorial for those who fought in the Boer War. A later memorial to those who fought in the World Wars has since been erected nearby.

THE QUARRY 1911

The Quarry Gardens are so-called because so much of the stone used to build early Shrewsbury was quarried here. The area dug out now forms a large lake and is the centrepiece in the town's park. Today the gardens are the venue for the annual Shrewsbury Flower Show, held regularly for over one hundred years.

THE WAR MEMORIAL 1911 63236

THE QUARRY 1911 63237

BOTTOM AVENUE, THE QUARRY 1896 38092

BOTTOM AVENUE
The Quarry 1896
In 1946 the not-yet-famous gardener, Percy Thrower, became Shrewsbury's Park Superintendent. He immediately upset everyone in the town by chopping down a nearby avenue of lime trees. They were diseased and unsafe, after all. Now, over fifty years later, the new trees he planted have grown to form a new avenue.

♦

THE QUARRY 1891 28945
Shrewsbury was one of the first towns in the country, as long ago as the 1700s, to set aside an area of land as a municipal garden. It is therefore no wonder that Shrewsbury sees itself as 'the town of flowers'. The top of the bandstand can be seen amongst the trees.

THE QUARRY 1891 28945

THE DINGLE, THE QUARRY 1923 73825

THE DINGLE
The Quarry 1923

Anyone walking here today would think
the gardens have hardly changed at all.
Since these pictures were taken,
however, the statue has been moved to a
new position overlooking the lake. It is a
statue of Sabrina, an ancient goddess of
the River Severn.

◆

OLD TOWER ON TOWN WALLS 1911

This is the only surviving watch tower on
Shrewsbury's town walls, which were
built in the 13th century. The tower has
a mixed history - it was a watch maker's
workshop at one time, and in the 1860s
was converted into a house. Today it is
maintained by the National Trust.

OLD TOWER ON TOWN WALLS 1911 63251

MILK STREET 1911 63227

The smart car everyone is admiring is parked outside the Old Post Office Hotel. Do not think of it as a post office in the modern sense - it was where people bought tickets to travel 'by post', or on the stagecoach. Letters went this way too, which is why we often refer to them as 'post'.

THE LION HOTEL c1955 S125057

The Lion Hotel was built in the 1700s and, like many hotels of the time, ran its own regular stagecoach service to towns all over the country. In 1800 there would have been around 200 coach horses stabled in Shrewsbury each night; the ostlers used to wash them in the river in the evenings.

THE UNICORN HOTEL, WYLE COP 1891 28911

From here the climb up Wyle Cop looks deceptively gentle. The name is a fascinating blend of old Welsh and old English. 'Wyle' means the road up the hill, and 'cop' is the top, so here we have simply 'the road up the hill to the top'.

WYLE COP c1891 38099
It is fascinating to compare this photograph and the
next - so much is about to change. Some of the signs
are interesting - I like 'Miss Durham Court
Dressmaker'. Also we have evidence of improved rail
communications, with fresh fish being brought all the
way from Grimsby. Notice, especially, the boy
collecting water from the street pump.

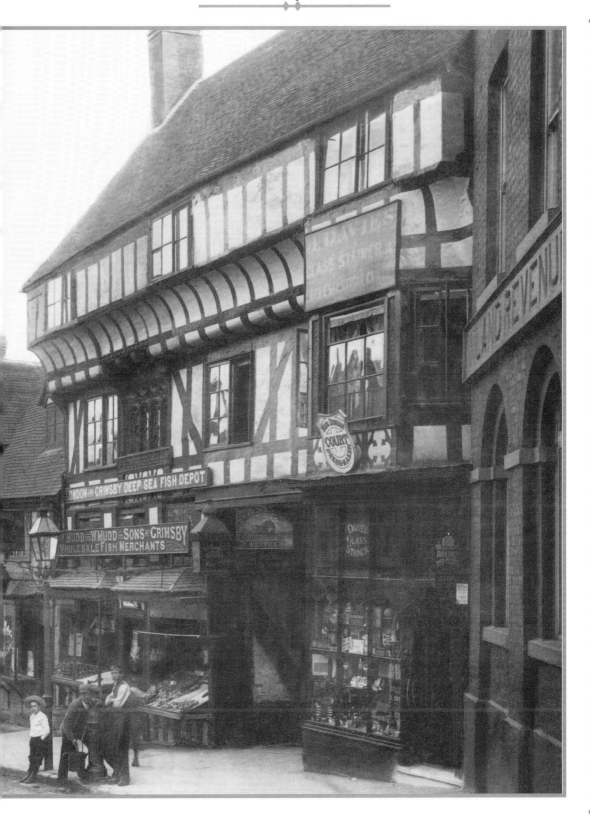

WYLE COP c1896 38099A

Today these buildings have hardly changed. The new building in the centre blends in well, but it is the others that are genuinely old. Harry Mudd's fish shop, behind the pump, dates to the 1430s. It is now known as Henry Tudor House - Henry VII stayed here on his way to fight Richard III at Bosworth Field.

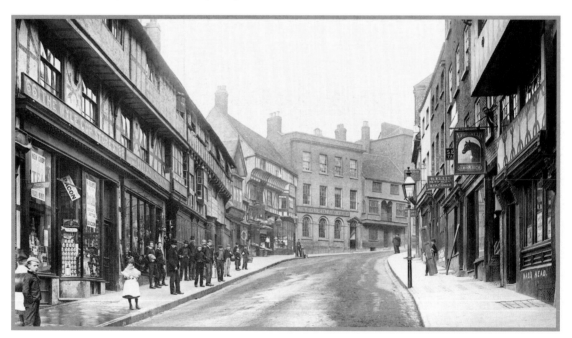

THE NAG'S HEAD 1891 28910

This is also Wyle Cop, but looking up the hill. Today the Inland Revenue Office is part of the Lion Hotel. Notice the young boy on the right taking down (or putting up) the shutters for the shop. Like everyone else, he still finds time to stop and stare at the photographer.

THE ENGLISH BRIDGE 1896 38093

'High the vanes of Shrewsbury gleam Islanded in Severn stream; The bridges from the steepled crest Cross the water east and west'. Just as AE Housman described it, the English Bridge crosses the water to the east of the town. It was built in 1774 by John Gwynne, who also designed the bridge at Atcham.

THE ENGLISH BRIDGE 1931 83873

Compare the gradient of the bridge in this picture with the photograph above - it is now slightly lower. This was done in 1927 to make it easier for modern traffic. The entire bridge was dismantled stone by stone, and the stones were reduced in height and then put back together again. At the same time the bridge was widened.

THE ENGLISH BRIDGE 1931 83875

A plaque on the bridge tells us that Queen Mary opened the bridge in 1927. Untrue. The official opening was cancelled at the last minute; but as Queen Mary had used the bridge on a recent private visit to the town, it was decided to say that it had then been officially opened by her.

THE INFIRMARY FROM THE RIVER 1903 49485

Overlooking the River Severn, the Infirmary (converted to shops and apartments now) sits on the site of a Dominican monastery. It was here that Prince Richard, the younger of the two Princes in the Tower, was born - he was to die in mysterious circumstances with his elder brother, Edward V.

VIEW NEAR THE RAILWAY BRIDGE 1891 28941

This picture gives an excellent impression of the swirl of the waters of the River Severn. In times of flood this footpath (which still exists) is always covered in water; sometimes the water can rise to levels well above the heads of the boys in the picture.

LAURA'S TOWER AND THE COUNCIL HOUSES FROM THE RIVER 1896 38091

The Council Houses were the chambers used by the President of the council in the Marches and his entourage when visiting Shrewsbury from their headquarters at Ludlow Castle. The complex of buildings dates from the 1500s, but was considerably altered in the 18th century. Since then they have been converted into private homes.

THE KINGSLAND BRIDGE 1896 38083

This bridge was built to link the new school site with the town. Originally it was a toll bridge for everyone; today pedestrians can cross for free, but drivers have to pay. Because of the height of both approaches it can be the only way into town when flood waters are high.

THE RIVER SEVERN 1911 63213

The Kingsland Bridge cost £11,156 to build in 1881. It was made by a company that constructed bridges all over the world, most notably the bridge below the Victoria Falls in Africa.

THE SCHOOL AND THE FERRY 1904
Shrewsbury School sits on a magnificent site overlooking the entire town of Shrewsbury. There were numerous points along the river where one could once cross by ferry. None exist today, although the post for this ferry, seen in the foreground, does still survive.

THE SCHOOL AND THE BOATHOUSE 1911
The school building was originally built in the 18th century to house orphans. These children were then trained to work in the cotton mills. These days it seems harsh treatment; in those times it was considered very philanthropic, for such children were thus provided with a means of earning a living.

THE SCHOOL AND THE FERRY 1904 51354

THE SCHOOL AND THE BOATHOUSE 1911 63217

THE SCHOOL BOATHOUSE 1911 63217A

The publication of Jerome K Jerome's book 'Three Men in a Boat' in 1889 did a great deal to encourage rowing as a sport. To this day Shrewsbury School has a strong rowing tradition. This is the school's boathouse - notice all the canoes stacked on the left.

THE PENGWERN BOAT HOUSE 1891 28898

The sport of rowing was not just for boys at Shrewsbury School. Further upstream is a rival club, the Pengwern Rowing Club, for the townspeople. Its name comes from an early Welsh place name which is thought by some to be an early name for Shrewsbury, though this is disputed by most modern scholars.

THE RIVER AND THE SCHOOL 1923
Along with floods, the River Severn often suffers from severe droughts. In order to ensure that it was possible to row at all times of the year, the river levels were artificially raised by the building of a weir further downstream.

◆

ON THE RIVER SEVERN 1911
With the old town almost completely surrounded by the river, Shrewsbury's inhabitants today are extremely fortunate because of the open spaces to which they have such easy access. The walks along both sides of the river are very popular, especially in springtime when the banks on the town side are yellow with daffodils.

THE RIVER AND THE SCHOOL 1923 73818

ON THE RIVER SEVERN 1911 63211

THE RIVER SEVERN 1911 63215
In medieval times the river would have been littered with town rubbish and effluent. By 1911 things had considerably improved; since then the river has been properly cleaned, and wildlife that had disappeared is now returning - otters can now sometimes be seen near this spot.

THE WELSH BRIDGE 1911 63220

A few hundred years ago this area would have been a hive of activity, with boatmen bringing goods up from Bristol and overseas and reloading with cloth and wool to take downstream. It has been estimated that, in terms of the numbers of boats using it, the river was one of the busiest in Europe.

THE BOATHOUSE INN 1911 63218

Notice the ferryman pulling on the rope in order to take his passengers across the river. Each passenger would have paid 1/2d for the ride.

THE PORTHILL SUSPENSION BRIDGE 1923 73831

Taken from almost the same position as the photograph opposite, this picture shows the bridge built in 1923 to replace the ferry. It cost £2,600; most of this money was donated by the Shropshire Horticultural Society, using profits raised from their annual flower show.

VIEW FROM PORTHILL SUSPENSION BRIDGE 1923 73834
With the newly built bridge offering free passage across the river the ferry, seen here moored to the river bank, is now redundant. Notice how the houses further along have their own access to the river.

THE WELSH BRIDGE 1896 38094
When this bridge was first built, Thomas Telford remarked that it had been badly sited and would suffer from scouring by the river. Sure enough, the abutments soon needed strengthening. The medieval bridge that it replaced was a wonderful structure with gatehouses, a row of shops and even a public toilet on it.

OLD HOUSES, FRANKWELL 1891 28918

This is one of the earliest of Shrewsbury's suburbs, dating from immediately after the Norman conquest. It was settled by people who, living outside the town's jurisdiction, avoided paying town rates. Notice 'Morris & Co': it was in Frankwell that they started trading - the sign on the wall is for their oil and candle works.

FRANKWELL 1911 63257

The same street some twenty years later, and hardly a thing has changed. The children standing in the middle of the road to watch the photographer could not do that now, however. Notice the butcher on the right standing outside his shop with haunches of meat hanging up beside him.

FRANKWELL 1911 63258
Trade was obviously quiet that day: our
butcher can still be seen in this photograph,
which looks along the street in the opposite
direction. The cobbler's sign in the window
on the right rather grandly advertises his
premises as 'The Frankwell Boot and Shoe
Repairing Depot'.

FRANKWELL 1911 63256

Today there is a large roundabout on this site. But the
building has not entirely disappeared - it was taken
down in the 1960s and reassembled in Bromsgrove at
the Avoncroft Museum of Buildings, where it now
houses the museum's shop and offices.

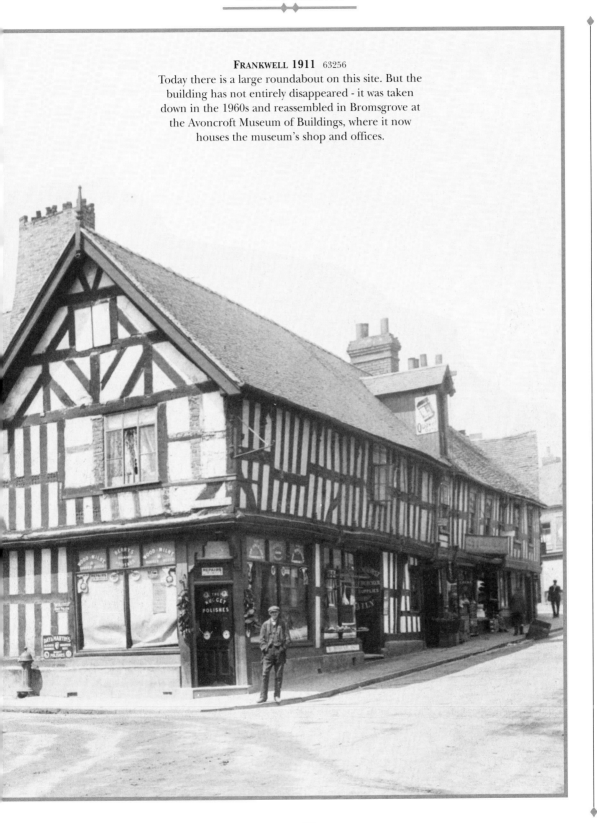

PORTHILL, KINGSLAND 1891 28951

PORTHILL, KINGSLAND 1891

Today Kingsland is a smart residential suburb very close to Shrewsbury's town centre. In medieval times the area was used as common land for the people of the town to graze their animals, and at one time it was also the place of execution for the town's criminals.

FROM THE SCHOOL 1891

The view from Shrewsbury School towards the town is superb. Here, on the skyline, we can see the cupola of St Chad's, the clock tower of the Victorian market hall, the steeples of St Alkmund's and St Mary's and Laura's Tower. Notice the sweep of the Kingsland Bridge on the right.

FROM THE SCHOOL 1891 28893

THE SCHOOL 1891 28903

Shrewsbury School originally occupied the present library in the heart of the town; it moved to its new site in Kingsland in 1882. Here it took over a former orphanage and workhouse - something that I am sure is considered very apt by all the schoolboys who have since passed through its gates.

THE SCHOOL 1896 38088

Today Shrewsbury School is still considered one of the best in the country, and there are many old boys whose names are well known to the public. They are quite a mixed collection - people such as Michael Heseltine and Nick Hancock, Willie Rushton and John Peel, Richard Ingrams and Michael Palin.

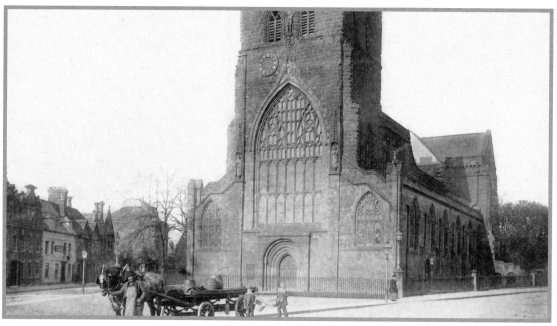

THE ABBEY CHURCH 1891 28927

Shrewsbury Abbey was founded by Roger de Montgomery in 1083. He was one of William the Conqueror's generals, and built many castles, but the abbey is his best memorial. Inside there is an early tomb that is reputed to be his - he died three days after becoming a monk in the abbey he founded.

THE ABBEY CHURCH FROM THE SOUTH-WEST 1924 76182

The Abbey was dissolved in the reign of Henry VIII, and much was then demolished - to the right it is possible to see the jagged wall where the cloisters were once attached. Fortunately, the western end had always served as the local parish church, which is the only reason why the church was allowed to survive.

THE ABBEY CHURCH 1891 28928

In the 19th century the abbey was restored and a new chancel added. Although it is easy to pick out the new work on the outside, internally it is much harder to distinguish old from new. Here we can see the solid round early Norman columns with the later Victorian work around the altar.

THE ABBEY FROM THE SOUTH 1896 38870

In medieval times Shrewsbury Abbey became extremely wealthy because it housed the shrine of the very popular St Winifred. Today pilgrims still come, but they are more likely to be seeking signs of Brother Cadfael, the (fictional) detective monk created by the writer Ellis Peters, whose exploits take place in 12th-century Shropshire.

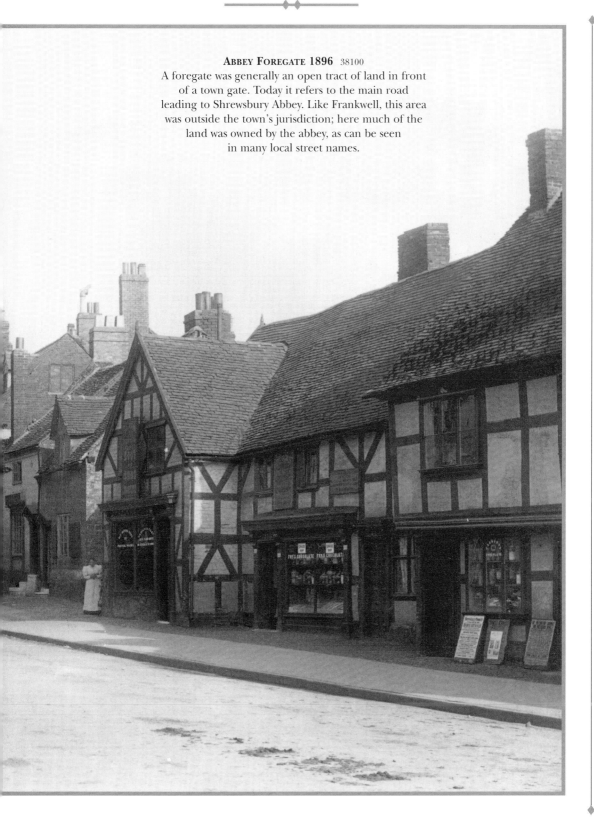

ABBEY FOREGATE 1896 38100
A foregate was generally an open tract of land in front
of a town gate. Today it refers to the main road
leading to Shrewsbury Abbey. Like Frankwell, this area
was outside the town's jurisdiction; here much of the
land was owned by the abbey, as can be seen
in many local street names.

LORD HILL'S MONUMENT 1891 28947

LORD HILL'S MONUMENT 1891
Lord Rowland Hill was a general in the early 1800s. He made his reputation in the Peninsular War and at the Battle of Waterloo. This is the largest Grecian Doric column in the world at 133' 6" (including the statue); there are 172 steps inside leading to a magnificent view of the town.

THE WOODLANDS
Youth Hostels Association c1960
This photograph must have been taken by someone who had climbed Lord Hill's column. The YHA was founded in Germany in 1907 by a teacher, Richard Schirrmann. The first hostels were opened in England in 1930.

THE WOODLANDS, YOUTH HOSTELS ASSOCIATION c1960 S125066

St Giles' Church 1891 28948
Now well within the town's suburbs, St Giles' was originally outside the town boundaries and served as a leper hospital in medieval times. St Giles was the patron saint of lepers; he was also patron saint to blacksmiths and nursing mothers - an unusual combination!

ATCHAM, THE BRIDGE AND THE CHURCH 1891 28958
Today Shrewsbury's town council is called the 'Shrewsbury
and Atcham Borough Council', for it includes the village of
Atcham some three miles away. The village grew up beside
a ford across the River Severn. The 18th-century bridge is
no longer safe for traffic, but survives as a footbridge
beside a new road bridge.

ATCHAM, THE CHURCH 1891 28960

ATCHAM
The Church 1891

The church is dedicated to St Eata, a 7th-century missionary who settled here to convert the pagan Anglo-Saxons. He gave his name not just to the church but to the village as well - the name means 'the homestead of the followers of Eata'.

◆

WROXETER
The Ruined Bathhouse c1864

It is amazing to consider that this was once a thriving Roman town predating Saxon Shrewsbury. Altogether it covered an area of around 180 acres, with defensive banks and ditches around the settlement running about 2 miles in length. Abandoned in the 6th century, most of the site now lies under fields.

WROXETER, THE RUINED BATHHOUSE c1864 2188

Index

Frith Book Co Titles

Frith Book Company publish over a 100 new titles each year. For latest catalogue please contact Frith Book Co

own Books 96pp, 100 photos. County and Themed Books 128pp, 150 photos (unless specified) All titles hardback laminated case and jacket except those indicated pb (paperback)

Around Barnstaple	1-85937-084-5	£12.99
Around Blackpool	1-85937-049-7	£12.99
Around Bognor Regis	1-85937-055-1	£12.99
Around Bristol	1-85937-050-0	£12.99
Around Cambridge	1-85937-092-6	£12.99
Cheshire	1-85937-045-4	£14.99
Around Chester	1-85937-090-X	£12.99
Around Chesterfield	1-85937-071-3	£12.99

Around Maidstone	1-85937-056-X	£12.99
North Yorkshire	1-85937-048-9	£14.99
Around Nottingham	1-85937-060-8	£12.99
Around Penzance	1-85937-069-1	£12.99
Around Reading	1-85937-087-X	£12.99
Around St Ives	1-85937-068-3	£12.99
Around Salisbury	1-85937-091-8	£12.99
Around Scarborough	1-85937-104-3	£12.99
Scottish Castles	1-85937-077-2	£14.99
Around Sevenoaks and Tonbridge	1-85937-057-8	£12.99
Sheffield and S Yorkshire	1-85937-070-5	£14.99
Shropshire	1-85937-083-7	£14.99
Staffordshire	1-85937-047-0 (96pp)	£12.99
Suffolk	1-85937-074-8	£14.99
Surrey	1-85937-081-0	£14.99
Torbay	1-85937-063-2	£12.99
Wiltshire	1-85937-053-5	£14.99

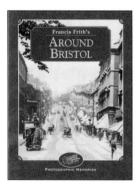

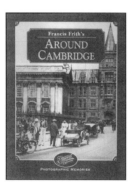

Around Chichester	1-85937-089-6	£12.99
Cornwall	1-85937-054-3	£14.99
Cotswolds	1-85937-099-3	£14.99
Around Derby	1-85937-046-2	£12.99
Devon	1-85937-052-7	£14.99
Dorset	1-85937-075-6	£14.99
Dorset Coast	1-85937-062-4	£14.99
Around Dublin	1-85937-058-6	£12.99
East Anglia	1-85937-059-4	£14.99
Around Eastbourne	1-85937-061-6	£12.99
English Castles	1-85937-078-0	£14.99
Around Falmouth	1-85937-066-7	£12.99
Hampshire	1-85937-064-0	£14.99
Isle of Man	1-85937-065-9	£14.99

British Life A Century Ago

246 x 189mm 144pp, hardback. Black and white Lavishly illustrated with photos from the turn of the century, and with extensive commentary. It offers a unique insight into the social history and heritage of bygone Britain.

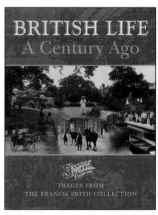

1-85937-103-5 £17.99

Available from your local bookshop or from the publisher

Around Bakewell	1-85937-1132	£12.99	Feb
Around Bath	1-85937-097-7	£12.99	Feb
Around Belfast	1-85937-094-2	£12.99	Feb
Around Bournemouth	1-85937-067-5	£12.99	Feb
Cambridgeshire	1-85937-086-1	£14.99	Feb
Essex	1-85937-082-9	£14.99	Feb
Greater Manchester	1-85937-108-6	£14.99	Feb
Around Guildford	1-85937-117-5	£12.99	Feb
Around Harrogate	1-85937-112-4	£12.99	Feb
Hertfordshire	1-85937-079-9	£14.99	Feb
Isle of Wight	1-85937-114-0	£14.99	Feb
Around Lincoln	1-85937-111-6	£12.99	Feb
Margate/Ramsgate	1-85937-116-7	£12.99	Feb
Northumberland and Tyne & Wear			
	1-85937-072-1	£14.99	Feb
Around Newark	1-85937-105-1	£12.99	Feb
Around Oxford	1-85937-096-9	£12.99	Feb
Oxfordshire	1-85937-076-4	£14.99	Feb
Around Shrewsbury	1-85937-110-8	£12.99	Feb
South Devon Coast	1-85937-107-8	£14.99	Feb
Around Southport	1-85937-106-x	£12.99	Feb
West Midlands	1-85937-109-4	£14.99	Feb
Cambridgeshire	1-85937-086-1	£14.99	Mar
County Durham	1-85937-123-x	£14.99	Mar
Cumbria	1-85937-101-9	£14.99	Mar
Down the Severn	1-85937-118-3	£14.99	Mar
Down the Thames	1-85937-121-3	£14.99	Mar
Around Exeter	1-85937-126-4	£12.99	Mar
Around Folkestone	1-85937-124-8	£12.99	Mar
Gloucestershire	1-85937-102-7	£14.99	Mar
Around Great Yarmouth			
	1-85937-085-3	£12.99	Mar
Kent Living Memories	1-85937-125-6	£14.99	Mar
Around Leicester	1-85937-073-x	£12.99	Mar
Around Liverpool	1-85937-051-9	£12.99	Mar
Around Plymouth	1-85937-119-1	£12.99	Mar
Around Portsmouth	1-85937-122-1	£12.99	Mar
Around Southampton	1-85937-088-8	£12.99	Mar
Around Stratford upon Avon			
	1-85937-098-5	£12.99	Mar
Welsh Castles	1-85937-120-5	£14.99	Mar
Canals and Waterways	1-85937-129-9	£17.99	Apr
East Sussex	1-85937-130-2	£14.99	Apr
Exmoor	1-85937-132-9	£14.99	Apr
Farms and Farming	1-85937-134-5	£17.99	Apr
Around Horsham	1-85937-127-2	£12.99	Apr
Ipswich (pb)	1-85937-133-7	£12.99	Apr
Ireland (pb)	1-85937-181-7	£9.99	Apr
London (pb)	1-85937-183-3	£9.99	Apr
New Forest	1-85937-128-0	£14.99	Apr
Scotland	1-85937-182-5	£9.99	Apr
Stone Circles & Ancient Monuments			
	1-85937-143-4	£17.99	Apr
Sussex (pb)	1-85937-184-1	£9.99	Apr
Colchester (pb)	1-85937-188-4	£8.99	May
County Maps of Britain			
	1-85937-156-6 (192pp)	£19.99	May
Around Harrow	1-85937-141-8	£12.99	May
Leicestershire (pb)	1-85937-185-x	£9.99	May
Lincolnshire	1-85937-135-3	£14.99	May
Around Newquay	1-85937-140-x	£12.99	May
Nottinghamshire (pb)	1-85937-187-6	£9.99	May
Redhill to Reigate	1-85937-137-x	£12.99	May
Scilly Isles	1-85937-136-1	£14.99	May
Victorian & Edwardian Yorkshire			
	1-85937-154-x	£14.99	May
Around Winchester	1-85937-139-6	£12.99	May
Yorkshire (pb)	1-85937-186-8	£9.99	May
Berkshire (pb)	1-85937-191-4	£9.99	Jun
Brighton (pb)	1-85937-192-2	£8.99	Jun
Dartmoor	1-85937-145-0	£14.99	Jun
East London	1-85937-080-2	£14.99	Jun
Glasgow (pb)	1-85937-190-6	£8.99	Jun
Kent (pb)	1-85937-189-2	£9.99	Jun
Victorian & Edwardian Kent			
	1-85937-149-3	£14.99	Jun
North Devon Coast	1-85937-146-9	£14.99	Jun
Peak District	1-85937-100-0	£14.99	Jun
Around Truro	1-85937-147-7	£12.99	Jun
Victorian & Edwardian Maritime Album			
	1-85937-144-2	£14.99	Jun
West Sussex	1-85937-148-5	£14.99	Jun

FRITH PRODUCTS & SERVICES

Francis Frith would doubtless be pleased to know that the pioneering publishing venture he started in 1860 still continues today. More than a hundred and thirty years later, The Francis Frith Collection continues in the same innovative tradition and is now one of the foremost publishers of vintage photographs in the world. Some of the current activities include:

Interior Decoration

Today Frith's photographs can be seen framed and as giant wall murals in thousands of pubs, restaurants, hotels, banks, retail stores and other public buildings throughout the country. In every case they enhance the unique local atmosphere of the places they depict and provide reminders of gentler days in an increasingly busy and frenetic world.

Product Promotions

Frith products have been used by many major companies to promote the sales of their own products or to reinforce their own history and heritage. Brands include Hovis bread, Courage beers, Scots Porage Oats, Colman's mustard, Cadbury's foods, Mellow Birds coffee, Dunhill pipe tobacco, Guinness, and Bulmer's Cider.

Genealogy and Family History

As the interest in family history and roots grows world-wide, more and more people are turning to Frith's photographs of Great Britain for images of the towns, villages and streets where their ancestors lived; and, of course, photographs of the churches and chapels where their ancestors were christened, married and buried are an essential part of every genealogy tree and family album.

A series of easy-to-use CD Roms is planned for publication, and an increasing number of Frith photographs will be able to be viewed on specialist genealogy sites. A growing range of Frith books will be available on CD.

The Internet

Already thousands of Frith photographs can be viewed and purchased on the internet. By the end of the year 2000 some 60,000 Frith photographs will be available on the internet. The number of sites is constantly expanding, each focussing on different products and services from the Collection.
Some of the sites are listed below.

www.townpages.co.uk
www.icollector.com
www.barclaysquare.co.uk
www.cornwall-online.co.uk

For background information on the Collection look at the three following sites:

www.francisfrith.com
www.francisfrith.co.uk
www.frithbook.co.uk

Frith Products

All Frith photographs are available Framed or just as Mounted Prints, and can be ordered from the address below. From time to time other products - Address Books, Calendars, Table Mats, Postcards etc - are available.

The Frith Collectors' Guild

In response to the many customers who enjoy collecting Frith photographs we have created the Frith Collectors' Guild. Members are entitled to a range of benefits, including a regular magazine, special discounts and special limited edition products.

For further information: if you would like further information on any of the above aspects of the Frith business please contact us at the address below:
The Francis Frith Collection, Frith's Barn, Teffont, Salisbury, Wiltshire England SP3 5QP.
Tel: +44 (0) 1722 716 376 Fax: +44 (0) 1722 716 881 Email: uksales@francisfrith.com

To receive your FREE Mounted Print

Cut out this Voucher and return it with your remittance for £1.50 to cover postage and handling. Choose any photograph included in this book. Your SEPIA print will be A4 in size, and mounted in a cream mount with burgundy rule lines, overall size 14 x 11 inches.

Order additional Mounted Prints at HALF PRICE (only £7.49 each*)

If there are further pictures you would like to order, possibly as gifts for friends and family, acquire them at half price (no additional postage and handling required).

Have your Mounted Prints framed*

For an additional £14.95 per print you can have your chosen Mounted Print framed in an elegant polished wood and gilt moulding, overall size 16 x 13 inches (no additional postage and handling required).

---

* IMPORTANT!
These special prices are only available if ordered using the original voucher on this page (no copies permitted) and at the same time as your free Mounted Print, for delivery to the same address

---

Frith Collectors' Guild

From time to time we publish a magazine of news and stories about Frith photographs and further special offers of Frith products. If you would like 12 months FREE membership, please return this form.

Send completed forms to:
The Francis Frith Collection, Frith's Barn, Teffont, Salisbury, Wiltshire SP3 5QP

Voucher for FREE and Reduced Price Frith Prints

Picture no.	Page number	Qty	Mounted @ £7.49	Framed + £14.95	Total Cost
		1	Free of charge*	£	£
			£	£	£
			£	£	£
			£	£	£
			£	£	£
			£	£	£

	* Post & handling	£1.50
Book Title	**Total Order Cost**	£

Please do not photocopy this voucher. Only the original is valid, so please cut it out and return it to us.

I enclose a cheque / postal order for £ . . . .
made payable to 'The Francis Frith Collection'
OR please debit my Mastercard / Visa / Switch / Amex card

Number . . . .

Expires . . . . Signature . . . .

Name Mr/Mrs/Ms . . . .

Address . . . .

. . . .

. . . .

. . . . Postcode . . . .

Daytime Tel No . . . .   Valid to 31/12/01

The Francis Frith Collectors' Guild

Please enrol me as a member for 12 months free of charge.

Name Mr/Mrs/Ms . . . .

Address . . . .

. . . .

. . . .

. . . . Postcode . . . .

Free Print - see overleaf